Learning to Read, Step by Step!

Ready to Read **Preschool–Kindergarten**
• big type and easy words • rhyme and rhythm • picture clues
For children who know the alphabet and are eager to begin reading.

Reading with Help **Preschool–Grade 1**
• basic vocabulary • short sentences • simple stories
For children who recognize familiar words and sound out new words with help.

Reading on Your Own **Grades 1–3**
• engaging characters • easy-to-follow plots • popular topics
For children who are ready to read on their own.

Reading Paragraphs **Grades 2–3**
• challenging vocabulary • short paragraphs • exciting stories
For newly independent readers who read simple sentences with confidence.

Ready for Chapters **Grades 2–4**
• chapters • longer paragraphs • full-color art
For children who want to take the plunge into chapter books but still like colorful pictures.

STEP INTO READING® is designed to give every child a successful reading experience. The grade levels are only guides; children will progress through the steps at their own speed, developing confidence in their reading. The F&P Text Level on the back cover serves as another tool to help you choose the right book for your child.

Remember, a lifetime love of reading starts with a single step!

With love to Christopher,
my all-American boy
—C.C.

For Adrien
—Z.L.

Random House Books for Young Readers
An imprint of Random House Children's Books
A division of Penguin Random House LLC
1745 Broadway, New York, NY 10019
penguinrandomhouse.com
StepIntoReading.com
rhcbooks.com

Library of Congress Cataloging-in-Publication Data is available upon request.
ISBN 979-8-217-22437-1 (trade) — ISBN 979-8-217-22438-8 (lib. bdg.) —
ISBN 979-8-217-22439-5 (ebook)

Manufactured in the United States of America
10 9 8 7 6 5 4 3 2 1

This book has been officially leveled by using the F&P Text Level Gradient™ Leveling System.

The authorized representative in the EU for product safety and compliance is Penguin Random House Ireland, Morrison Chambers, 32 Nassau Street, Dublin D02 YH68, Ireland, https://eu-contact.penguin.ie.

STEP INTO READING®

A NON-FICTION READER

America

Our Country, Our Home

by Courtney Carbone
illustrated by Zhen Liu

Random House New York

Our country is
the United States
of America.

It was founded
in 1776.

Our Founding Fathers created a document called the Declaration of Independence.

It said we were free
from British rule!

America's birthday is
the Fourth of July.
That day is called
Independence Day.

We celebrate this holiday with parades and fireworks!

This is
the American flag.
It has
thirteen stripes
and fifty stars.

One star
for every state!

Our flag is even
on the moon!

The bald eagle
is a proud symbol
of our country.

A picture of this bird is found on our dollars and coins.

Our country is led
by a president.
The president lives
in the White House
in Washington, DC.

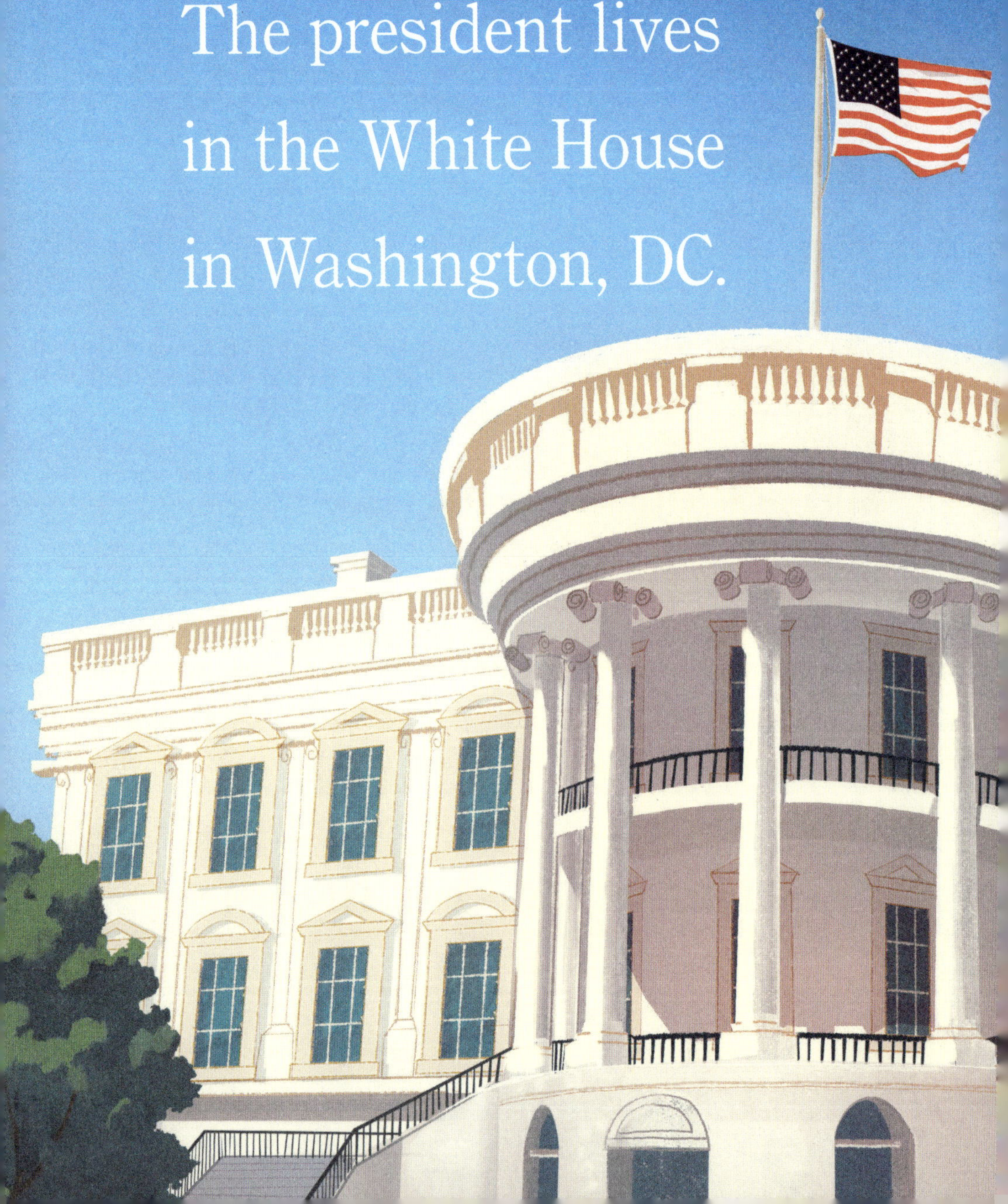

That is the capital
of the United States.
The capital is named
after our first president.

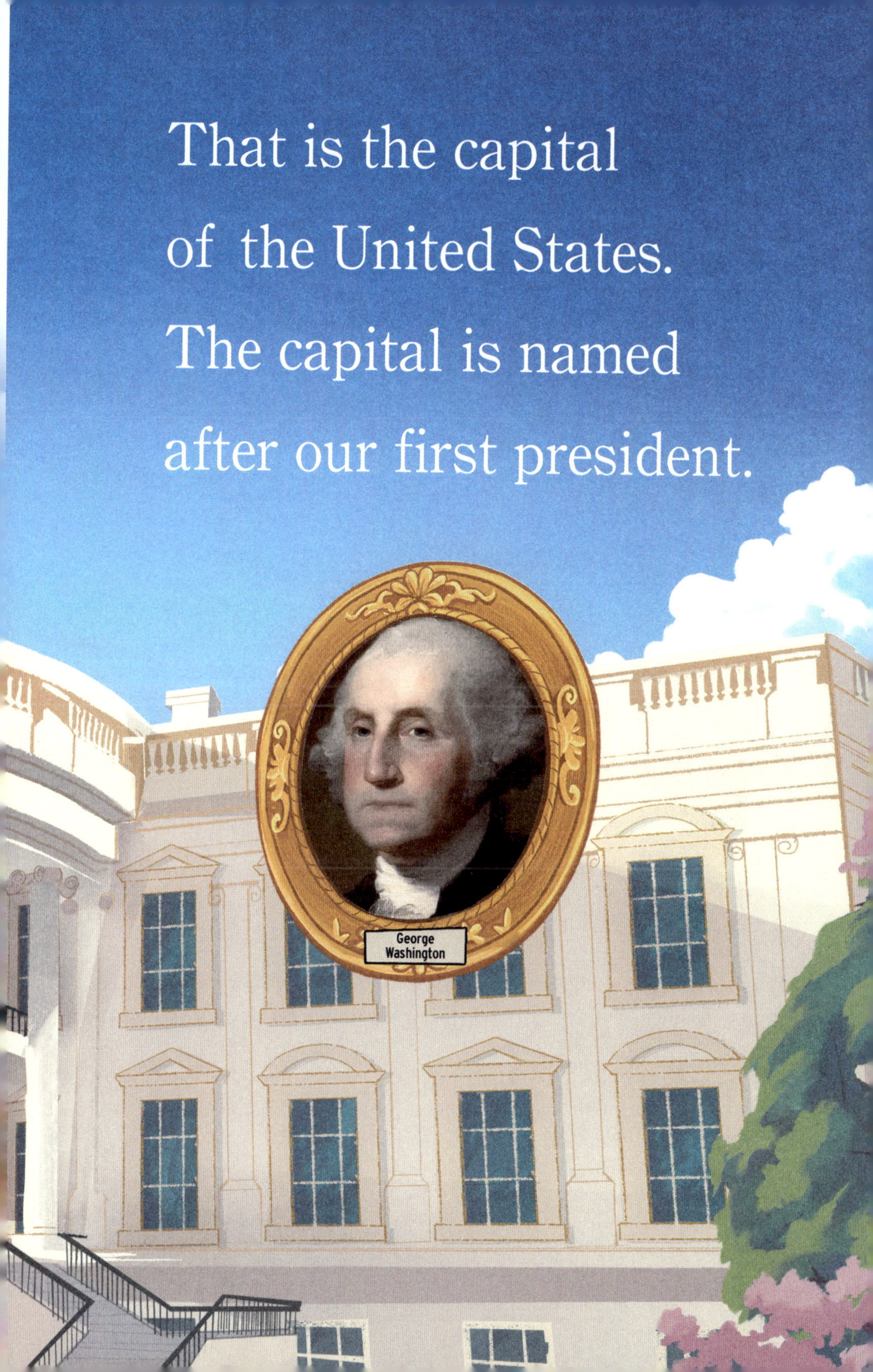

Laws are made
by people in Congress.
We elect the president
and Congress people
to represent us.

That is why voting is
so important!

The laws are written in the Constitution. Judges rule on these laws in court.

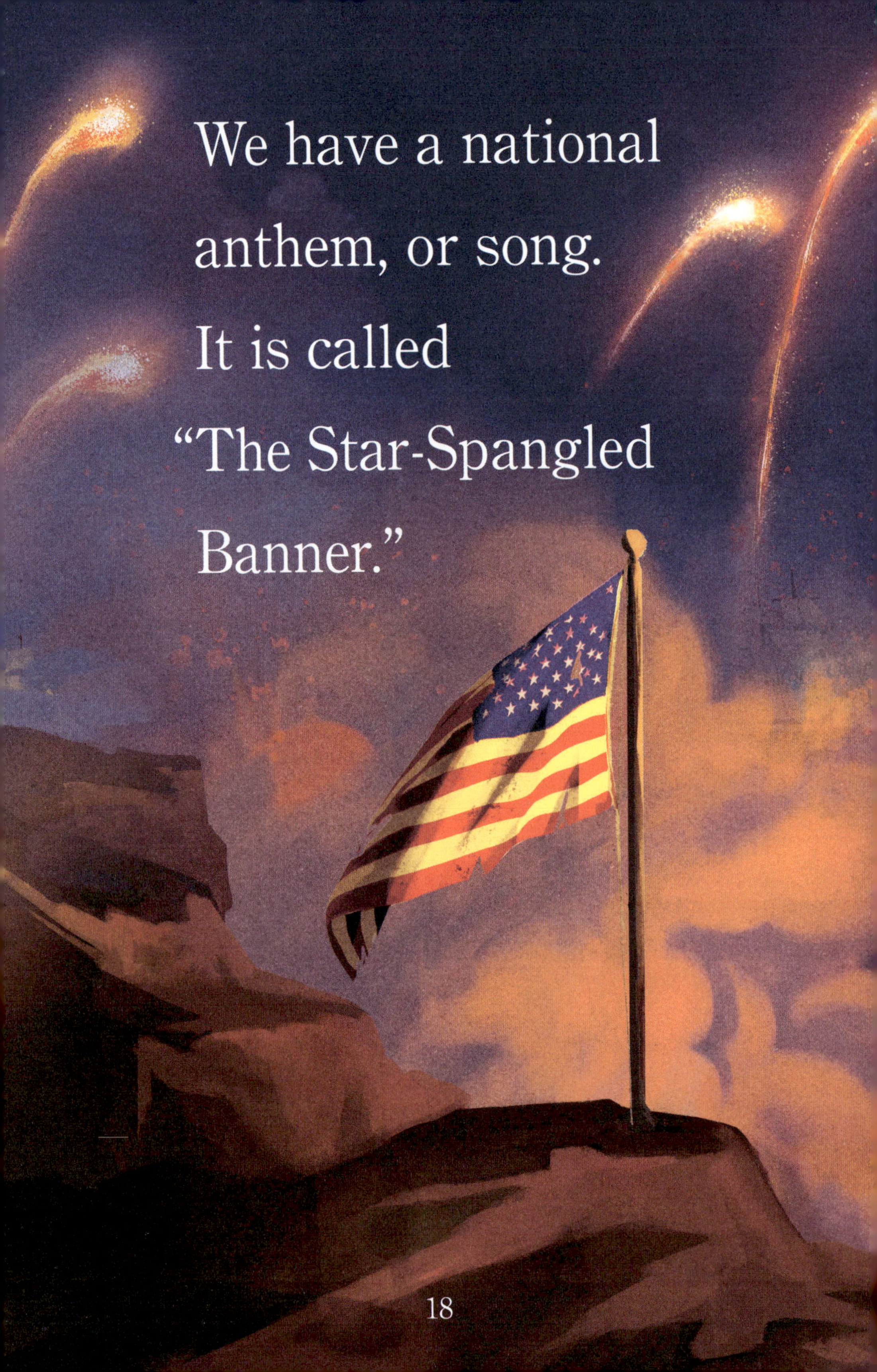

We have a national anthem, or song. It is called "The Star-Spangled Banner."

We also have
the Pledge of Allegiance.
We recite this pledge
as a sign of loyalty
to our country.

America has
many national parks.
They protect nature
and the land.

These parks are home
to wildlife
like plants and animals.

Our country is big!
It has many regions
and climates.
Some areas are hot.
Others are cold.
There are deserts,

forests,

grasslands,

and tundra.

We also have many landmarks. Some are natural.

Others were
made by humans.

People of
different races and
from all over the world
call America home.
Over 300 million people
live here!

Some live in cities.

Some live in small towns.

Some live on tribal lands.

Americans love
to get together
for food and fun.

We celebrate special times with family, friends, and neighbors. Yum!

America is known as the land of the free and the home of the brave.

We believe in liberty
and justice for all.
Now that is
something to celebrate!

Happy birthday, America!